Fabrizio Sa

C000108083

A VISUAL SCULPT

SIDE-VIEW PORTRAITS

198 photos explaining how to model side-view portraits in the relief engraving technique

2019

Translation   **Elena Cherubini**

Cover image   **Pamela Natalini – EXAGON GROUP**

SUMMARY

INTRODUCTION   PAG. 3

CLASSIFICATION OF THE HANDWORKS   PAG. 8

TOOLS AND MATERIALS   PAG. 11

CHOOSING THE CLAY   PAG. 13

PICTURES OF THE FACE   PAG. 13

PREPARING THE CLAY PLATE   PAG. 18

SIDE VIEW OF THE PORTRAIT   PAG. 35

BAKING   PAG. 114

INTRODUCTION

As I continue the sharing of my sculpting experiences, I will offer you three manuals dealing with the relief-engraving technique and I will teach you how to make a portrait.

I chose the theme of the portrait because, in its complexity, it represents an important milestone in the career of an artist who is dedicated to figurative arts.

Besides, when in your sculpting career you get to the point of properly sculpting a portrait, I can assure you that you will also be capable of sculpting any other subject well enough.

In the first manual we will discuss the side-view portrait, in the second the three-quarters portrait, and in the third the front-view portrait.

As for the difficulty, the most complex is the front-view portrait, following in descending order, the three-quarters portrait and the side-view portrait.

In terms of resemblance, the three-quarters portrait is the most effective, followed by the side-view and the front-view.

Therefore, we can say that for reasons of ease and resemblance, the side-view portrait has always been more successful than the others, and by consequence it has been the most used, as one can easily ascertain from the numerous examples in art history.

Dealing with these three kinds of portraits in a single volume would have meant using hundreds of pictures, which would have made the manual difficult to consult and, at the same time, excessively expensive.

For this reason, I considered it appropriate to divide everything in three separate volumes, even though they'll have common chapters and a separate section – the practical-realization one – which will be different every time.

There has always been some inaccuracy around handwork definition, as it is divided in only three categories: bas-reliefs, high reliefs e all-round. There are, in fact, other categories, which we will define in the next chapter.

In these three manuals we'll make portraits in the relief-engraving technique, where the figures have a thickness of a few millimeters.

When making this kind of reliefs, lighting is crucial. I'm not only talking about the lighting of the subject we mean to portray, which we'll cover later, but also the lighting of the workplace.

Since the portraits we're about to make will be - as I mentioned before – a few millimeters thick, in order to see the slightest differences well enough, it is extremely important to prepare a light source near the worktable, and place it a little bit higher than the worktable.

The light source, placed in this way, produces shadows on your engraved relief, which highlight its shapes and thicknesses in detail.

In the picture above we see the final handwork described in the first manual, which deals with side-view engraved portraits.

This picture shows the portrait dealt with in the second manual, which is the three-quarters-view portrait.

In this last picture we see the handwork covered in the third manual, which is the front-view portrait.

CLASSIFICATION OF HANDWORKS BY SHAPE

Since I often happen to hear wrong or inaccurate definitions regarding sculpture, I believe that, first of all, it's appropriate to give proper definitions in order to correctly classify our work.

Sculptural works are divided into two big categories: **relief** and **all-round.**

Reliefs. They are works that are inscribed on a clay plate of variable thickness and that have a variable thickness and depth. They can be considered a transition from painting to sculpture. Usually this expressive solution is used to represent complex scenes, that would be difficult to make in the all-round, for example scenes containing numerous subjects, landscapes, architectural elements etc.

Reliefs can in turn be divided in two categories: **sunk (or sunken) reliefs** and **proper reliefs.**

Sunk Reliefs We can use this term when the work is engraved in the thickness of the plate; the engraved figure doesn't exceed the plate in height and its borders are engraved in the plate with variable depth. In the past this technique was used in Egyptian art.

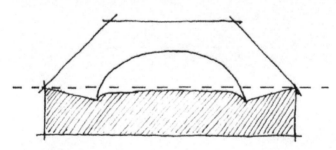

Representation of a sphere realized with
the sunk relief technique seen in section

Proper Reliefs

They can be defined according to the thickness of the figure on the plate.

Schiacciato or stiacciato (shallow) Relief. The figure realized on the plate has a slight thickness and the borders can be finely engraved on the plate.

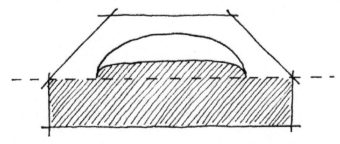

Representation of a sphere realized with the Schiacciato technique on a plate seen in section

Bas-relief (or Low relief). The figure realized on the plate must have a thickness that, coming out of the plate itself, does not exceed half of what would be its volume if it were made in the round.

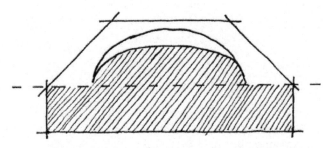

Representation of a sphere realized with the bas-relief technique on a plate seen in section

Mid-relief (or Half-relief). The figure realized on the plate must have a thickness that, coming out of the plate itself, is equal or slightly superior to half of its volume if it were made in the round.

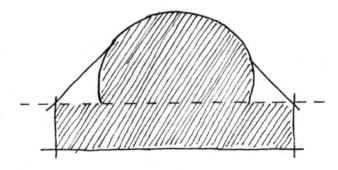

Representation of a sphere realized with a mid-relief technique on a plate seen in section

High Relief. The figure realized on the plate must have a thickness that, coming out of the plate itself, is equal or slightly inferior to its volume if it were made in the round. The figures are complete, even if they remain attached to the plate.

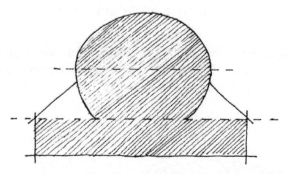

Representation of a sphere realized with the high relief technique on a plate seen in section

All Round. These are autonomous sculptures designed to be viewed from all sides. They are not attached to a plate.

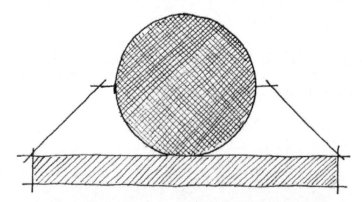

Representation of a sphere realized with the all-round technique on a plate seen in section

TOOLS AND MATERIALS

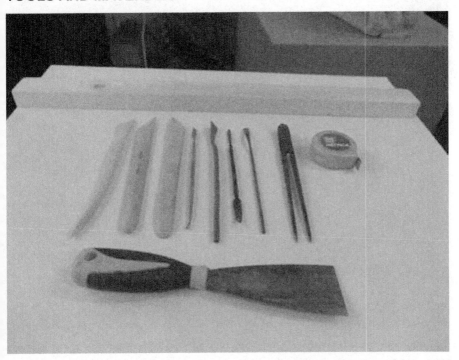

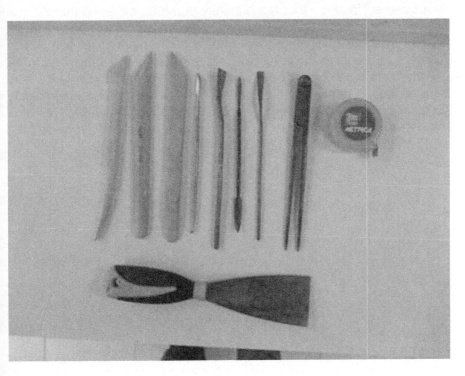

As you can see from the pictures, we will need spatulas, compasses, tape measure and a wooden board: I use a chipboard table with a plasticized surface, so that the humidity of the clay doesn't impregnate the wood, distorting it. We will also need a sheet of paper and a wooden rod to make the clay plate. The choice of the spatula is completely personal, depending on your own experience. Every one of you will already have his/her own collection of spatulas; my advice is to have some wooden ones to hew the shapes and some metal ones to refine the details. What is absolutely essential when making portraits is owning compasses of different sizes, which will be used to mark on the clay the anatomical measures taken from the picture of the face.

CHOOSING THE CLAY

To make any clay sculpture and therefore our portrait, which we will then bake in the oven at 970°C, it is absolutely necessary to use good refractory clay.

Refractory clay is a mixture made from clay and grains of ground ceramic, called CHAMOTTE. This mixture prevents excessive shrinking when drying and excessive expansion when baking and ultimately prevents cracking during these two stages.

There are refractory mixtures of various colors and percentages of chamotte, on the market. You can choose whichever one you like, with the colour that suits you best, but it is essential that the mixture contains a good percentage of chamotte (about 40%), and that it has a large enough grain size, not inferior to one millimeter and even better if it is 1,5 mm (the greater the quantity and the size of the chamotte grains contained in the clay, the greater the probability of avoiding cracking when baking).

PICTURES OF THE FACE

When making a portrait, it is often complicated if not impossible to have the subject available for the entire duration of the work, so it is useful to use pictures as a reference. In this course we will learn how to use some photographs of the subject we want to portray.

First of all, you need to get the most realistic pictures possible, without distortions caused by usage of not suitable digital tools, such as phones, tablets and cameras with poor efficiency, or incorrect framing.

Recommendations to obtain correct pictures:

1   You will need to take 3 pictures for every subject, one for every angle: front, right or left side, and one with a three-quarter view. Make sure that the subject maintains the same facial expression in all the positions.

2   The pictures must be taken all at the same height (approximately equal to the mouth) and all at the same distance from the face, about 1.5 / 2 meters.

3   Use a camera that has lenses that allows you to take pictures from the above mentioned distances and that, at the same time, can fill the frame. (ZOOM)

4   The illumination of the face must highlight the anatomical forms as much as possible. To that end, I recommend having the subject stand near a window, so that one side of the face is illuminated by the bright light of day but not directly by the sun, and the other side by a softer ambient light (you will need to do some tests until you get the best illumination).

5   If we want to make a life-size portrait sculpture it is advisable to print the photos in A3 format paper, I recommend using a graphic software that allows you to scale the three pictures as you see in the following examples.

In my opinion, it's sufficient to print the pictures in black and white: having colour in sculpture is not important.

 Attention, you will need two prints for each picture: two for the subject seen from the side, two for the face seen from three quarters and two for the subject seen from the front.

Below, we can see the pictures of the subject we will portray.

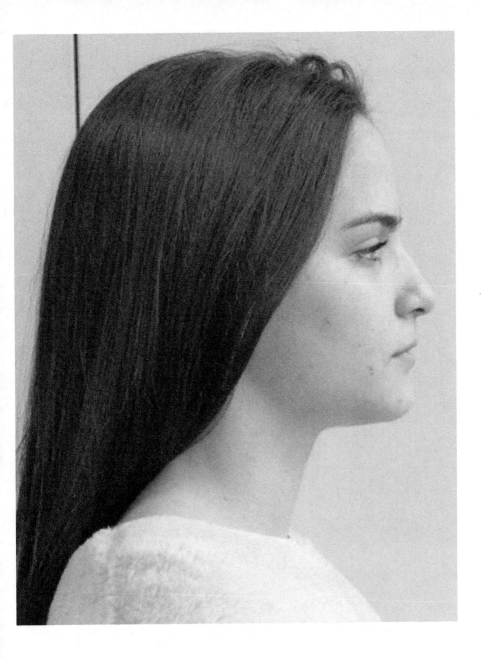

Subject seen from the side.

Notice how in the picture the light coming from the right is more intense and the ambient light is softer so that the shapes of the face are more evident.

Subject seen form three quarters.

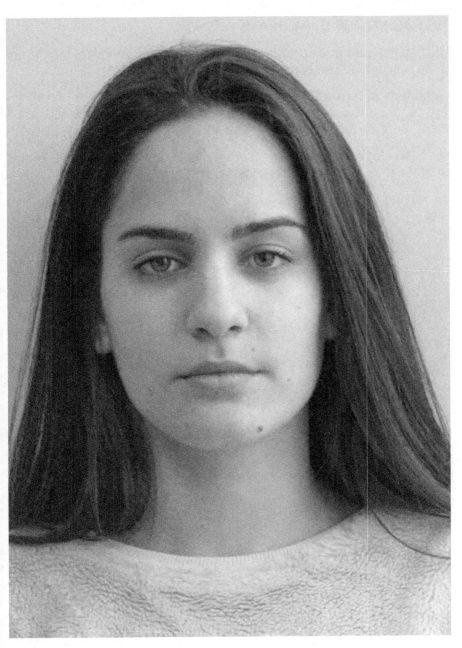

Subject seen from the front.

PREPARING THE CLAY PLATE

The first thing to do is to measure the height and the length of the picture of the subject, as you can see in the pictures below.

I recommend making the clay plate bigger than the picture, so that it has some space around it. I suggest increasing the size by at least 5 cm or more on each side.

For example, if the picture measures 25 x 30 cm, the clay plate should be at least 35 x 40 cm with a thickness of 3 cm.

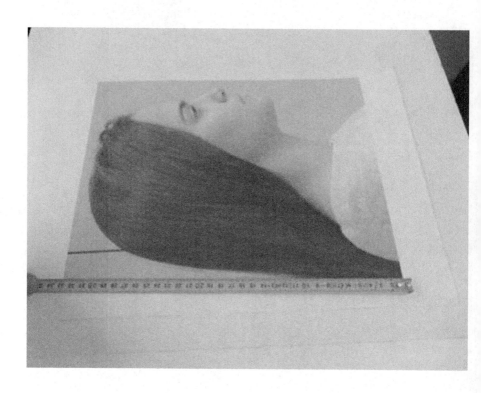

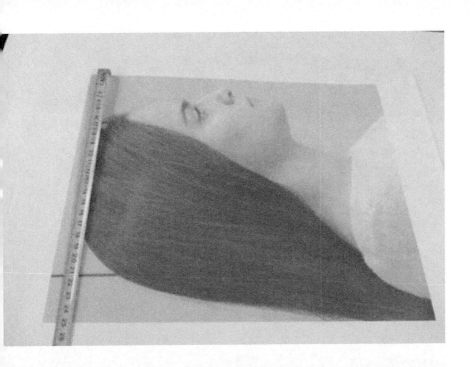

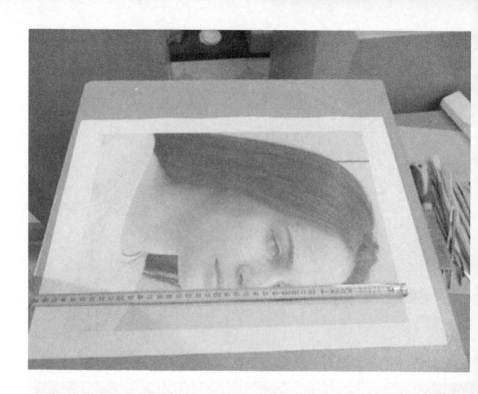

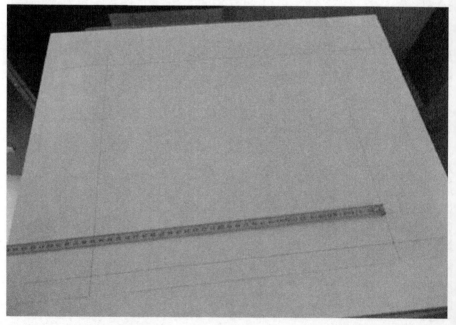

We place a sheet of paper on the workplace and with a pencil we trace a rectangle which will have the dimensions of the clay plate. The sheet of paper has the crucial function of preventing the clay from sticking to the workplace. As a matter of facts, as you will probably already know, when drying, the clay shrinks. If it stuck directly to the workplace it would not shrink and so it would break, irreparably ruining your creation.

I recommend extending the vertex marks at the corners of the rectangle as you can see in the pictures above. The reason will be explained later.

Place some loaves of clay on a support and with a spatula cut slices of about 4-5 cm in thickness, then place them inside the rectangle drawn on the paper.

As soon as you've filled the space with clay, start pressing with your fingers to amalgamate the pieces. Press well so that all the pieces are well joined and form a single body. Be careful, this operation is extremely important. Avoid creating gaps and empty spaces between the pieces, or they could create cracks when baking that would ruin all your work.

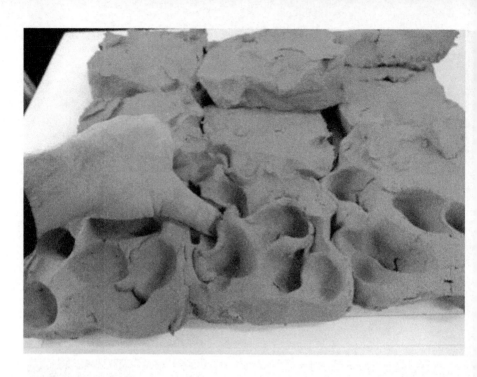

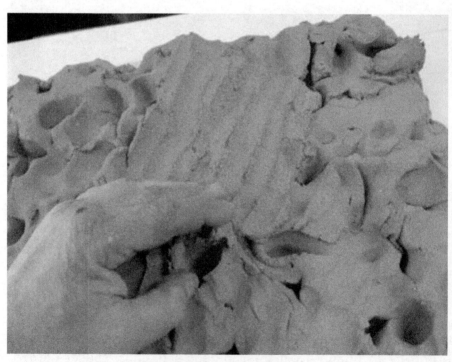

Try to level the plate as much as you can, first with fingers then with the spatula, as you can see in the pictures above and below.

At this point, measure the thickness of the plate. It should be about 3.5 cm on each side.

Take the wooden rod and place it with both hands on the clay plate, so that a smooth and sharp corner scrapes the surface of the clay as you pull towards yourself.

Repeat this operation until the plate is sufficiently smooth and devoid of bumps and holes. Every time, remove the clay stuck to the wooden rod.

If there still remain some hardly removable depressions, take some clay and fill them as you can see in the pictures above and below.

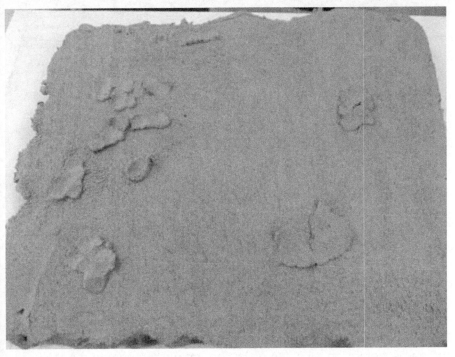

Take the wooden rod again and pull several times in different directions, this way you will get a perfectly smooth plate. Check that the plate has the same height on all sides. With the various scrapings the thickness should have reduced from 3,5 cm to 3 cm.

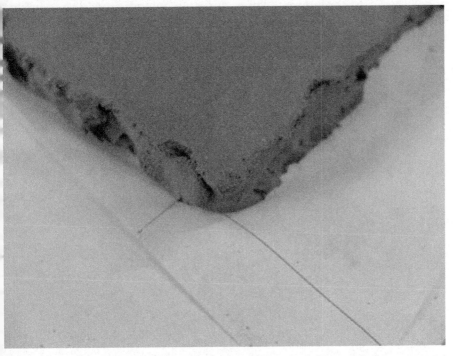

At this point you'll notice that the borders of the plate are irregular and exceed the rectangle on the piece of paper by a few centimeters. Now we'll have to trim the borders to ensure that they meet the dimensions set by the drawing.

Take the wooden rod again and gently place it on the clay plate at the pencil marks on the paper. With the spatula cut the excess clay, as you can see in the pictures above and below.

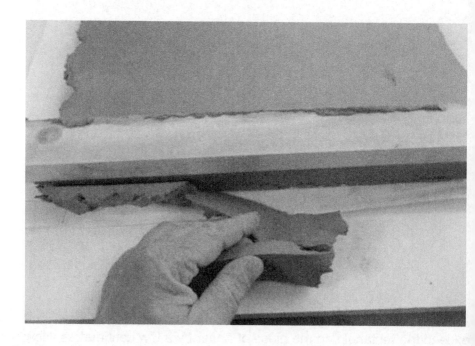

Repeat the operation on all the four sides. As you will have noticed, drawing longer lines on the corners of the rectangle turned out very useful for this trimming operation.

The clay plate is done and it is ready to be engraved.

SIDE-VIEW PORTRAITS

198 photos explaining how to model side-view portraits in the relief engraving technique

Now that we have the clay plate, the pictures printed in A3 format paper and the spatulas, we can finally start engraving our side-view portrait.

The first thing to do is to take one of the prints and place it on the fresh clay plate. Make sure your face is centered with respect to the plate, as you can see in the pictures below.

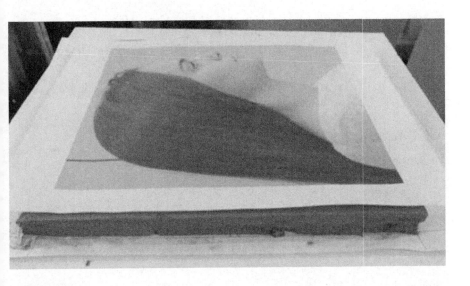

The next operation will have to be performed as quickly as possible because the fresh clay will wet the paper and for every minute the paper stays on the clay, it mollifies, swells, distorts and becomes more susceptible to tears.

Take a pointed spatula and try to go over the main lines of the face, as you can see below, by pressing lightly and keeping the tip inclined.

Going over with the tip not tilted but perpendicular, you risk tearing the already partially mollified paper. Retrace the contour of the whole head, the hair, the eyes and the ears if visible.

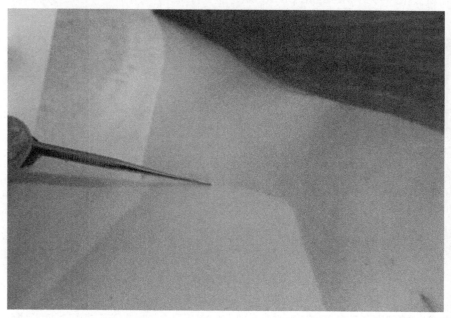

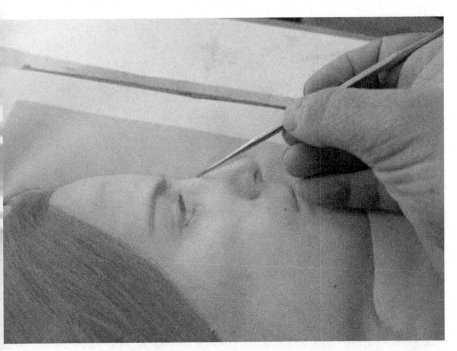

As soon as you finish, take out the picture and throw it away: you won't need it anymore ruined as it is. In the picture below you can observe the result of what you just did, you can see the contours of the traced head.

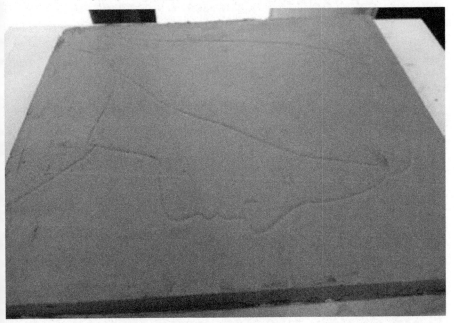

Since the marks are faint, I recommend retracing and highlighting them with the same pointed spatula as seen below.

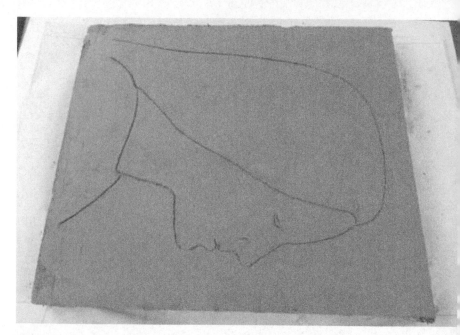

Next, we have to engrave the contour of the head, with a spatula in the form of a cutting blade, with a depth of about 8-10 mm. Two important recommendations: first of all, try to keep the same cutting depth for the whole contour and, secondly, always make sure that the cut is perpendicular to the plate. Without these two precautions the shapes of the face may vary their dimensions as we go along, compromising the verisimilitude. See pictures below.

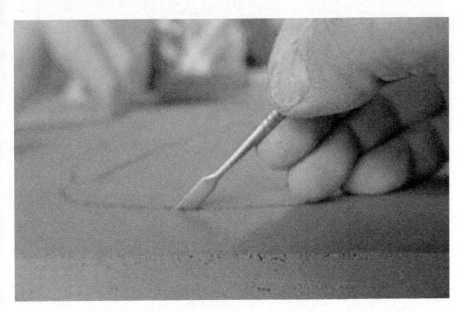

Right after you engrave the contours, you need to remove a layer of clay around the head, as you can see in the following pictures.

Take a spatula with a flat and sharp tip; slip it in the engraving and remove a layer of clay of about 8-10 mm.

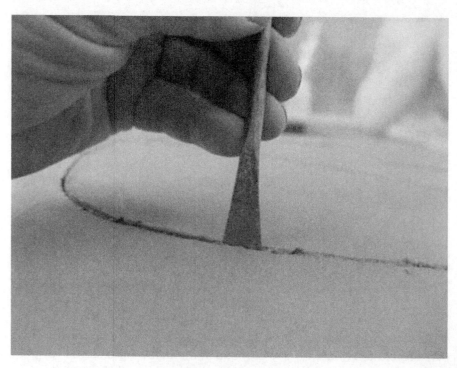

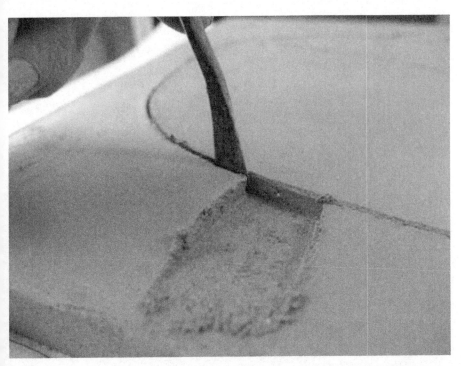

Insert the spatula in the incision in a perfectly vertical way (perpendicular to the clay plate) and pull outwards in order to form a sort of slide as shown in the picture above and below.

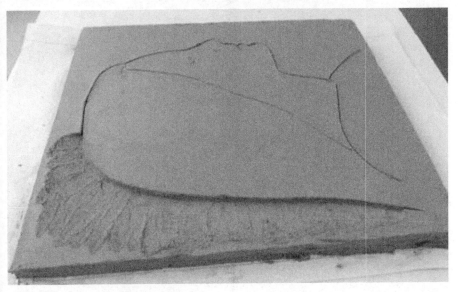

Do this all around the figure.

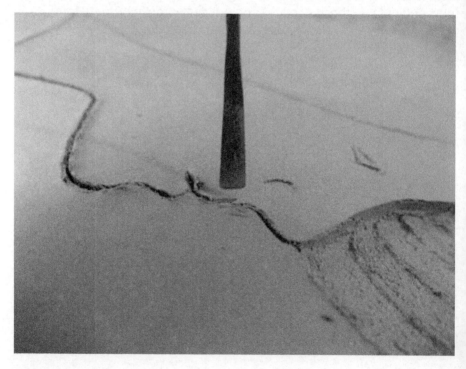

In the direction of the nose and mouth, where the details of the face are smaller, use a narrower spatula.

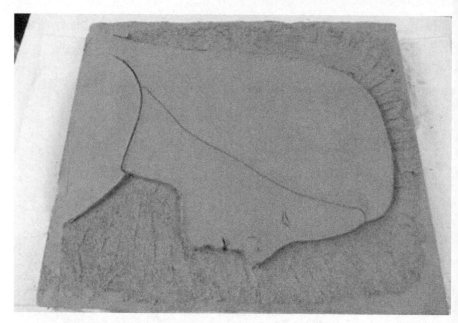

As you can see from the picture above, the shape of the head has been completely cropped.

The depth of the cropping starts from 8-10 millimeters in coincidence with the perimeter of the head and, as one goes outwards, it decreases until it becomes zero at the outer edges of the clay plate.

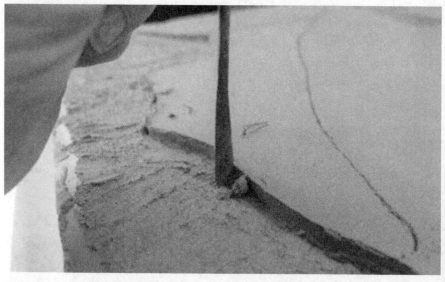

Immediately after cropping, it is necessary to adjust the contours of the figure, ensuring that the edge exactly matches the sign obtained previously by engraving the plate with the picture. Furthermore, the edge must also be 8-10 mm thick throughout the entire perimeter and

44

finally the edge must be perfectly vertical with respect to the plate as shown in the picture below.

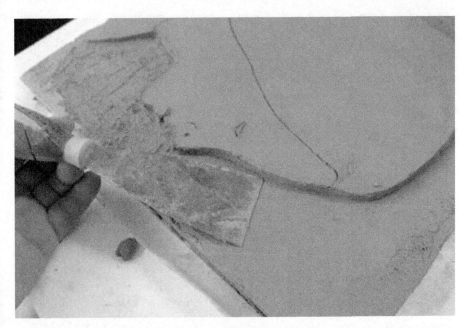

After arranging the edges as explained above, take the wide blade spatula and use it to smooth the entire surface around the shape of the head, as shown in the following pictures.

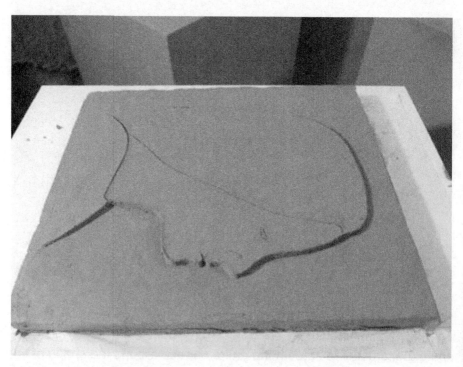

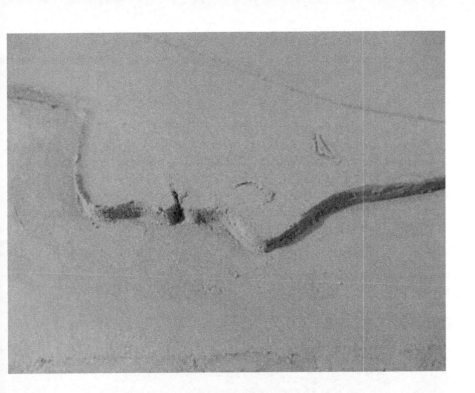

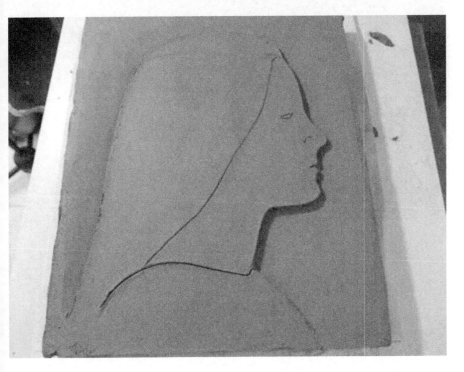

Now you have obtained the shape of the head that emerges from the clay plate by about 8-10 mm with the edges well defined and perpendicular to the plate.

You can finally start working on the face, but before you begin using the spatulas, I strongly suggest making a careful and meticulous check of the dimensions of the details of the face as shown in the following pictures. With the compass, measure the dimensions of the anatomical details in the picture and compare them with the corresponding clay part. Even a single millimeter of difference will compromise the verisimilitude of the portrait.

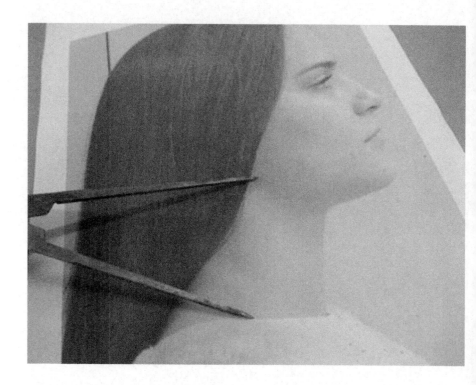

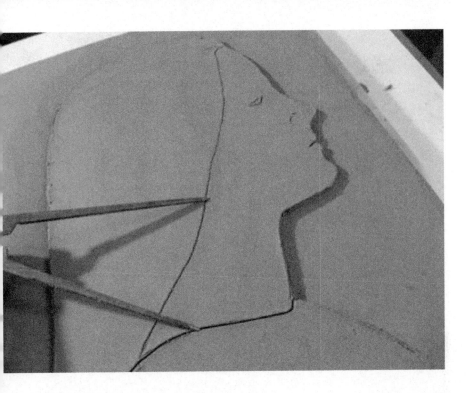

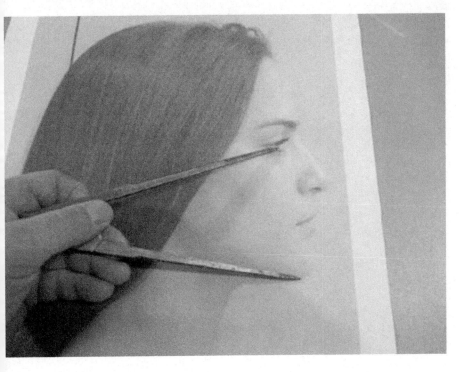

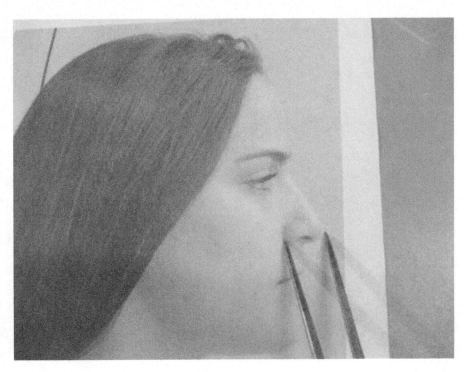

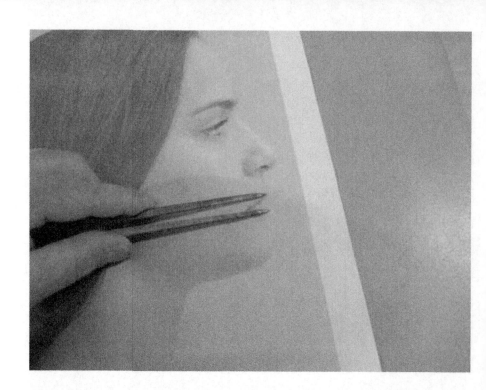

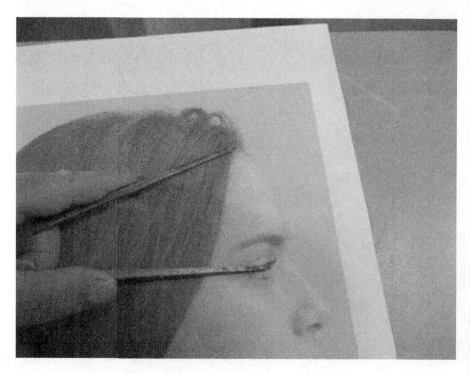

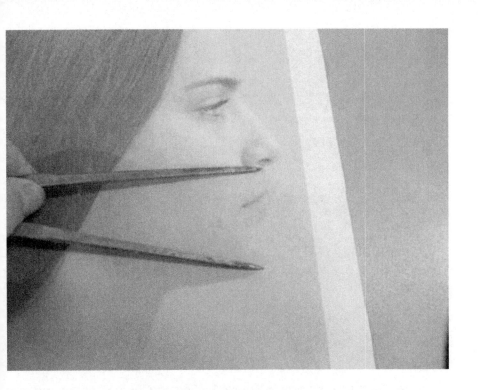

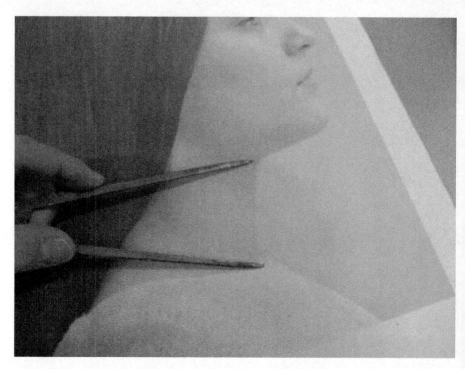

As soon as this meticulous check is finished, we can get out our spatulas. I would recommend starting with the neck. The neck, compared to the whole figure of the head, is one of the lowest parts from which it is therefore necessary to remove more clay.

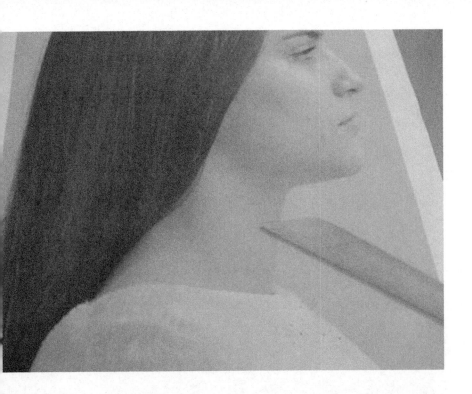

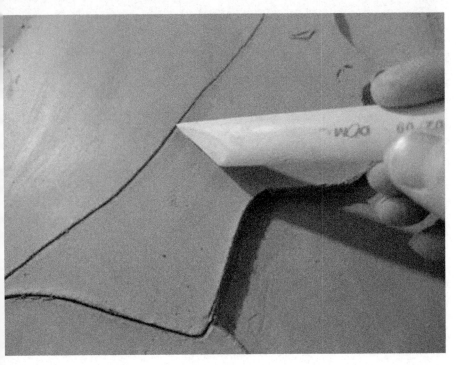

Start removing clay with the spatula as shown in the pictures below. If the neck emerges from the plate by 10 millimeters, remove clay until it emerges from the plate by a maximum of 3 millimeters.

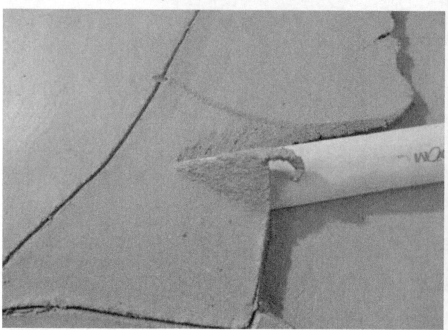

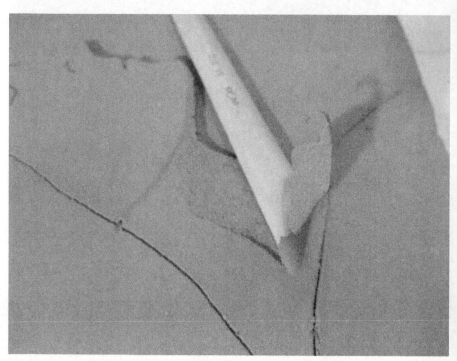

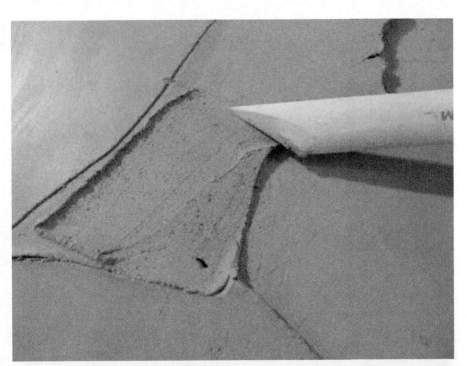

Immediately after removing the clay from the neck, remove some more from the edge of the head, sketching the shape of the nape and hair as shown in the pictures below.

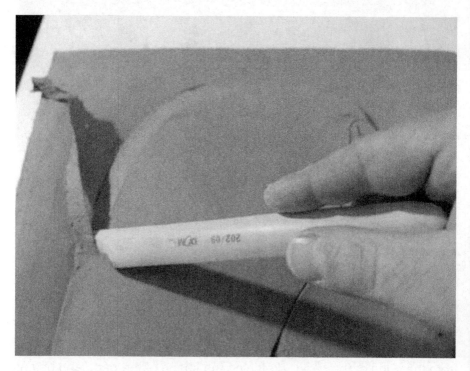

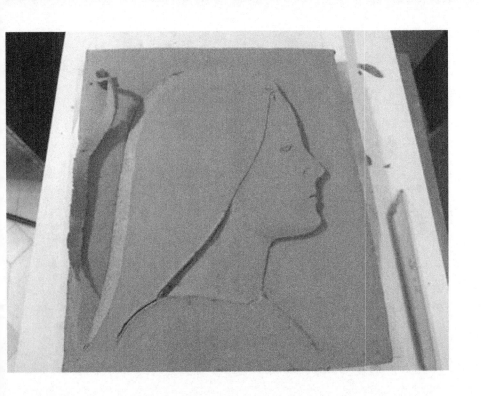

Once you have finished, move on to defining the shape of the shoulder and contextually the shape of the shirt and defining the neck. Follow the pictures below.

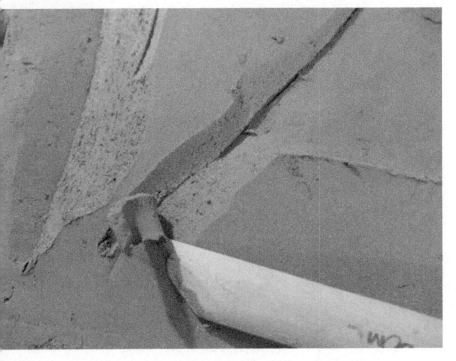

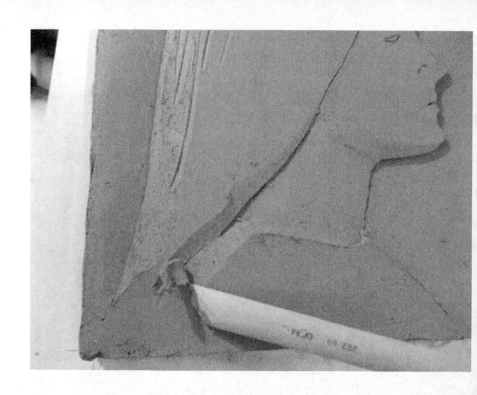

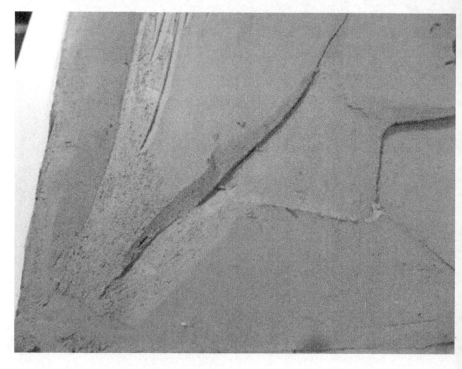

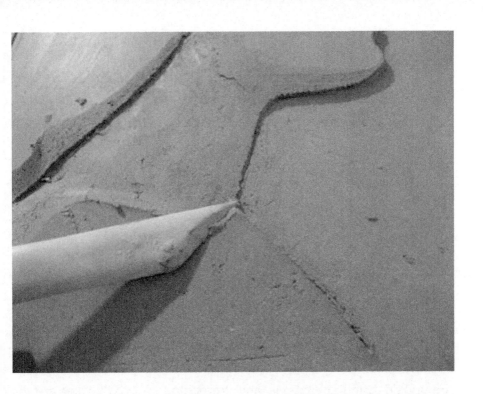

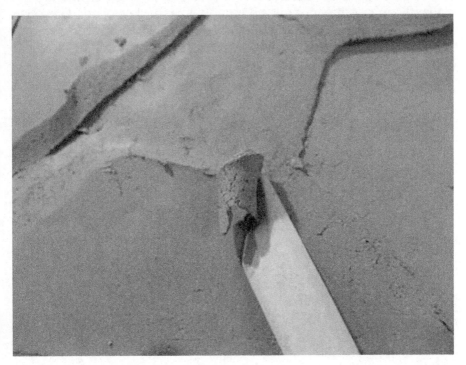

The shoulder, the cheekbone and the central part of the hair are the highest parts of the portrait compared to the clay plate. Obviously everything is based on the difference in thickness of a few millimeters and the skill of a good sculptor is based precisely on the ability to recreate the different depths in just a few millimeters of thickness.

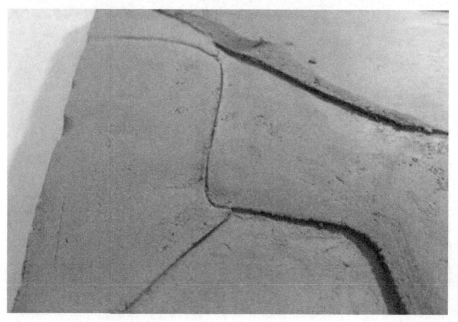

You will notice that when working, the surfaces are rough. This is due to the presence of chamotte mixed with clay (grains of cooked and ground clay that make sanding more difficult).

As soon as shoulder and neck are defined, you can summarily sketch the hair as shown in the following pictures.

In the picture above you can see that the hair is barely outlined and the surfaces of the neck and the shoulder are not yet perfectly smooth. With the final sanding, we will define the muscles of the neck as well.

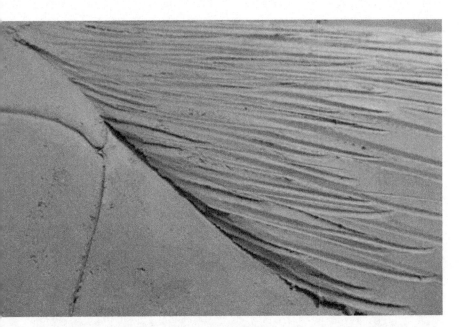

Now it's time to face the most important and challenging task, that is working on the face. However, don't worry: by following the pictures and suggestions below you will succeed perfectly.

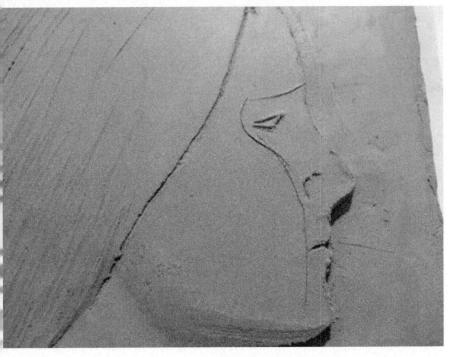

In the picture above I have traced a temporary line that starts from the eyebrow and goes down to the chin to indicate that everything that appears on the right side should be lowered by removing clay, as you can see in the following pictures.

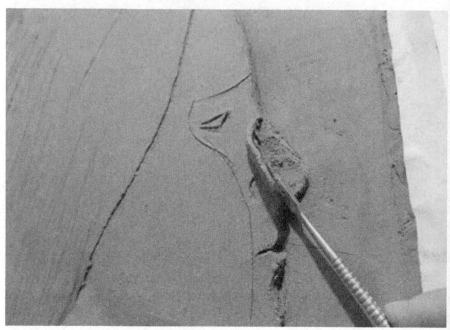

Start by removing clay from the nose.

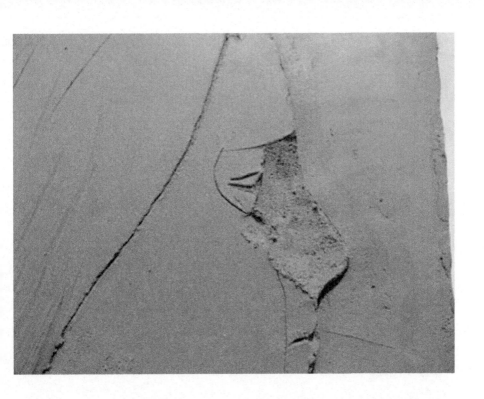

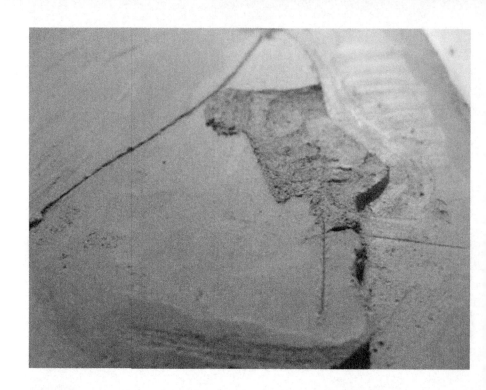

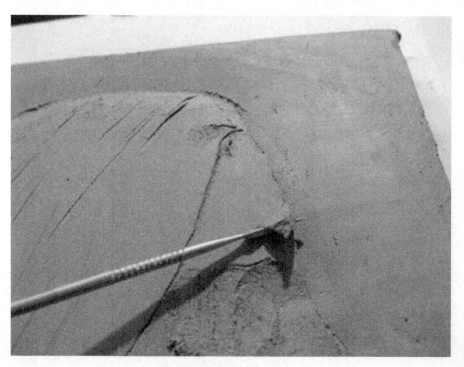

Remove clay from the edge of the forehead.

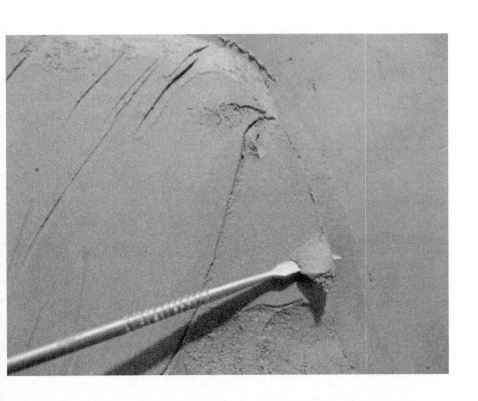

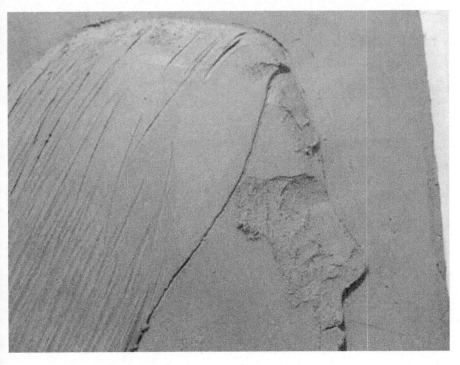

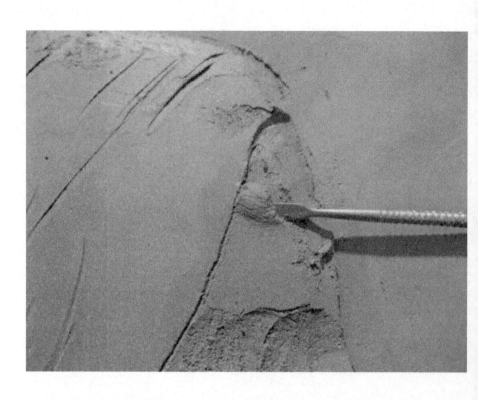

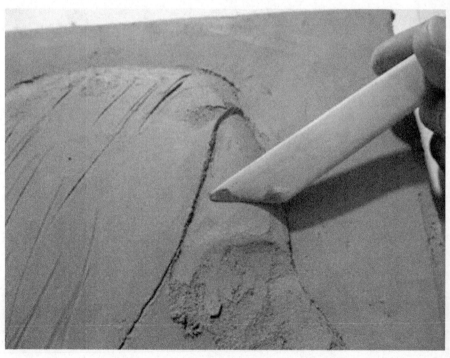

Remove clay at the borderline between the hair and the face as well:
lower it by about a millimeter.

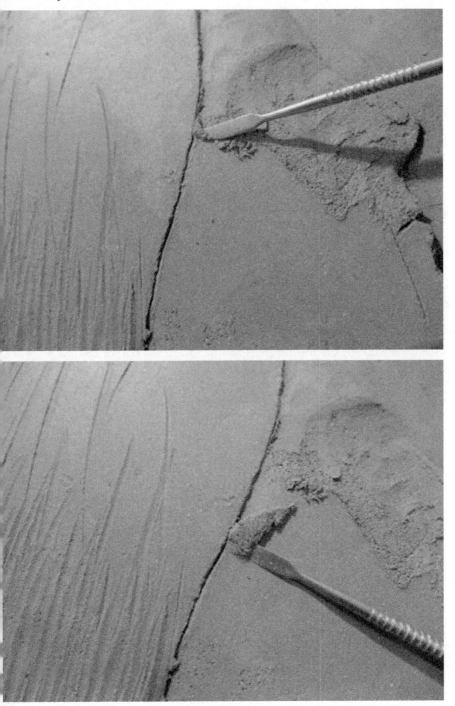

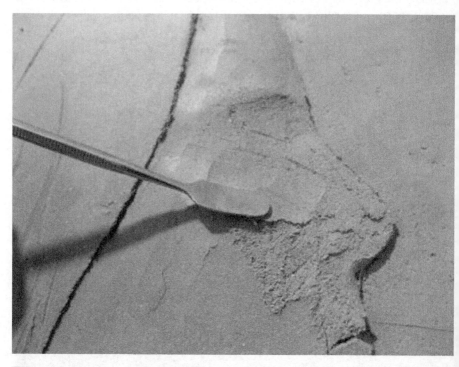

The cheekbone, on the other hand, is one of the highest parts of the whole portrait.

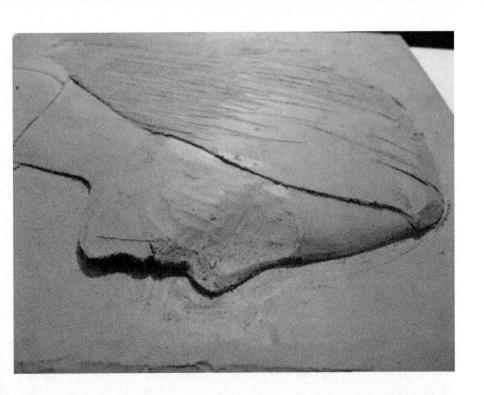

At this point the forehead, eyebrow and cheekbone are outlined.

Let's now move on to modeling the chin and the mouth, as shown in the following pictures.

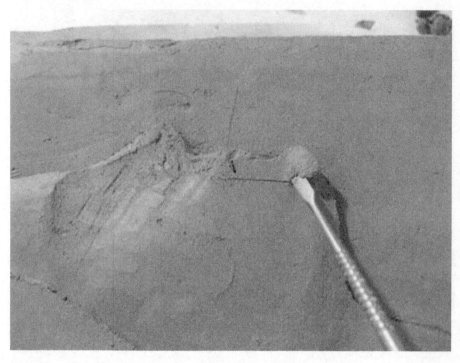

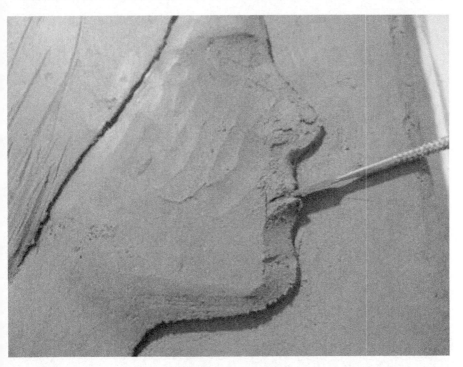

Before moving on to the details of the mouth, let's check the correct measurement with the compass, comparing the measurements observed in the picture with those in the clay.

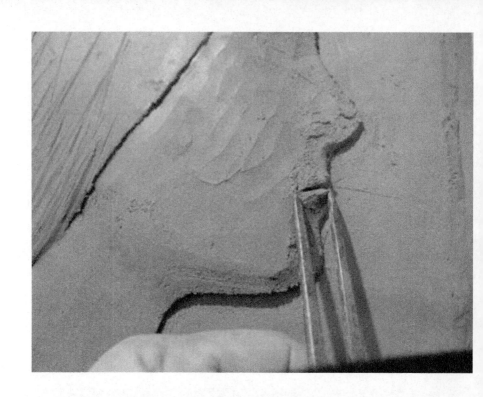

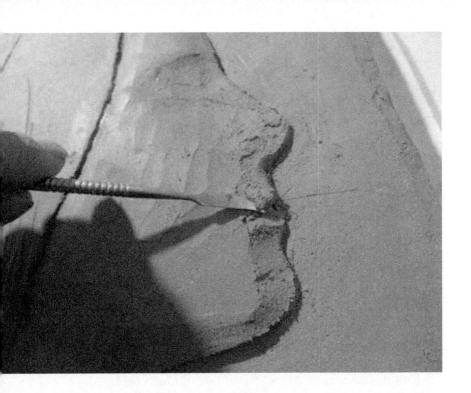

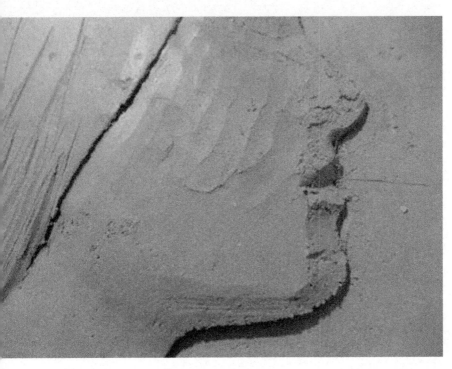

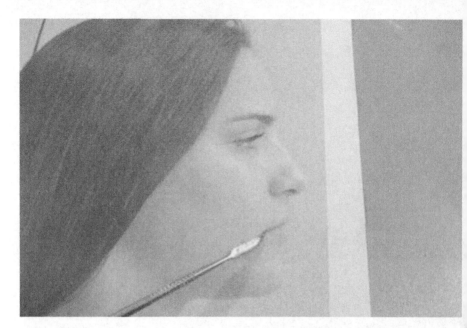

In the picture above the spatula indicates the point where the upper and lower lips are joined. In this area there is always a depression that is different depending on the age and sex of the subject.

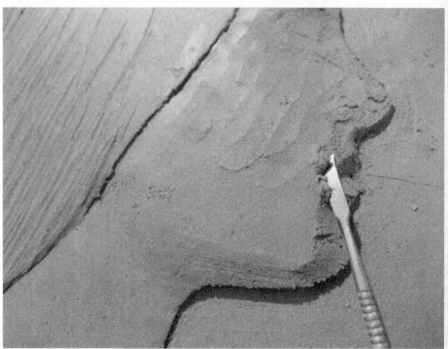

Remove some clay at the crossing of the lips.

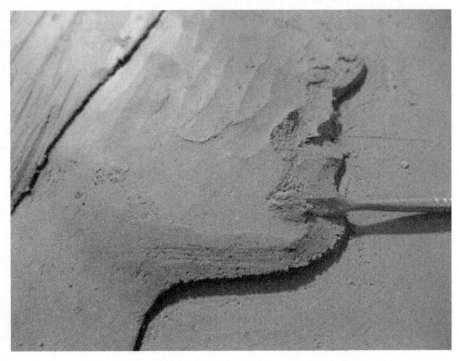

Define the chin more as shown in the following pictures.

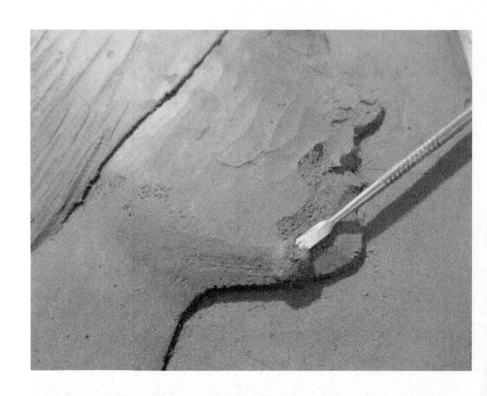

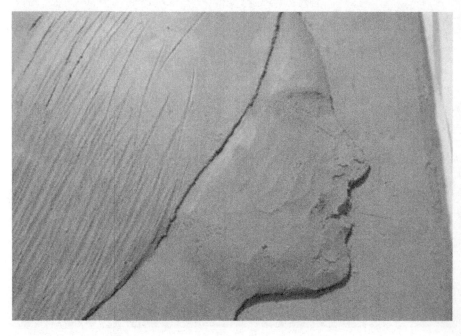

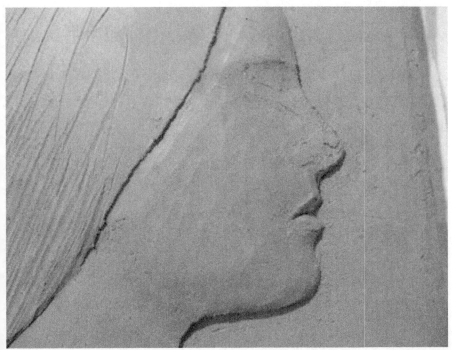

Define the lips more precisely. To facilitate this operation, compare the lips of the picture with the ones you are modeling.

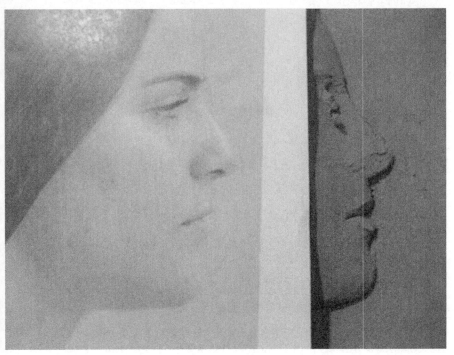

At this point, cheeks, chin, cheekbone and forehead have reached an almost final shape.

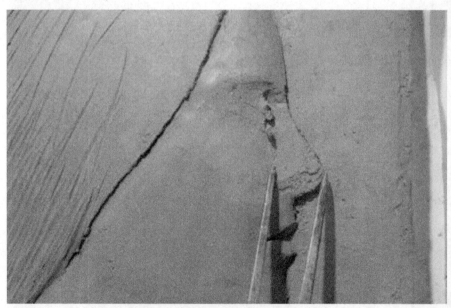

Let's move on to nose modeling. Before using the spatula, check with the compass the correct dimensions and position with respect to the other anatomical elements.

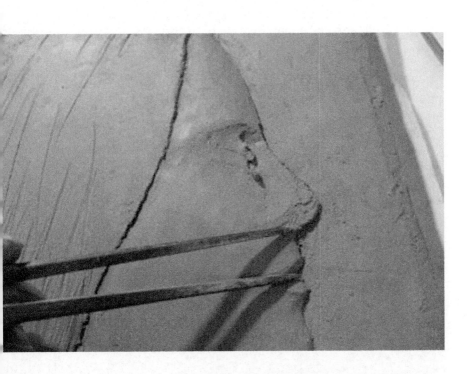

The nose is one of the lowest parts of the whole portrait, while the nostril will be about one millimeter higher than the nose. Follow the photos below.

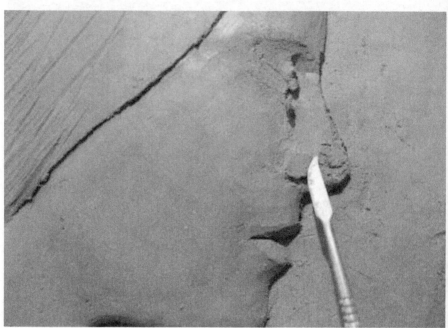

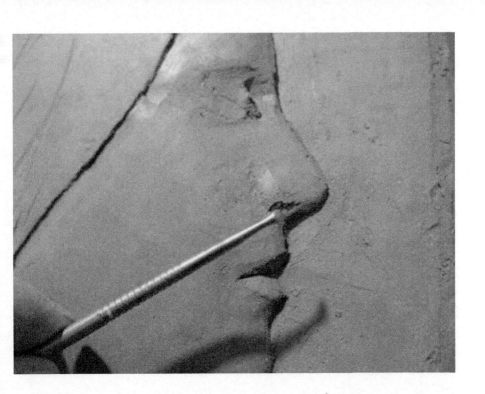

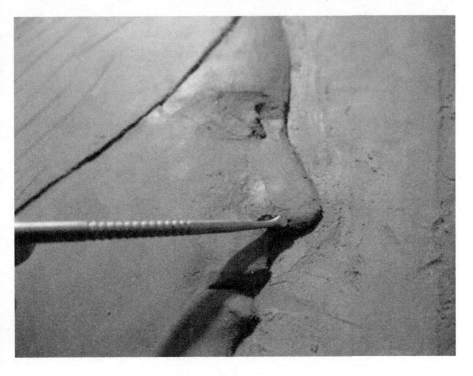

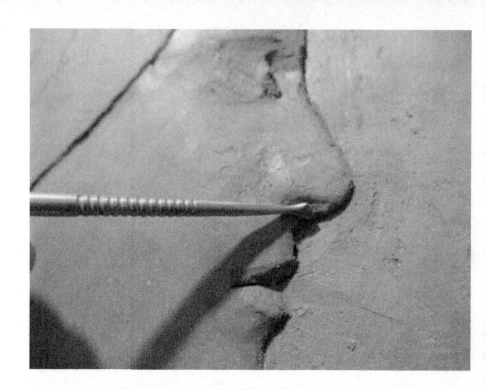

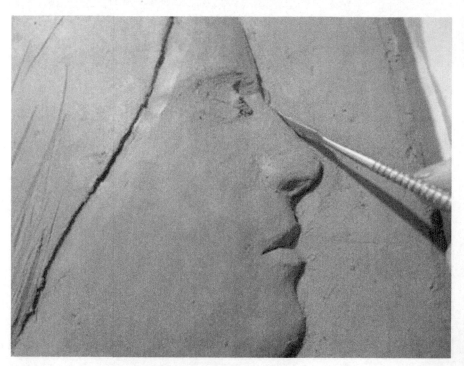

Define more accurately the edges of the nose.

Do for the nose as you did for the mouth, comparing it with the picture to reach the maximum verisimilitude. Pay attention to the profile of the nose, because in the side portrait this is decisive.

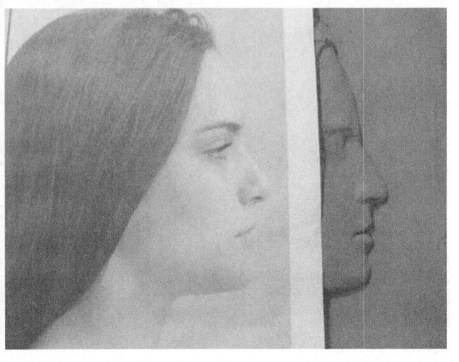

Now let's start modeling the eye.

At the point indicated with the spatula, the eyebrow has a bulge, present in all young females' faces.

Add some clay and spread it to form the bulge. See the pictures below.

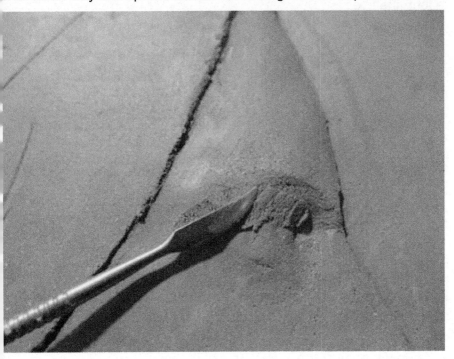

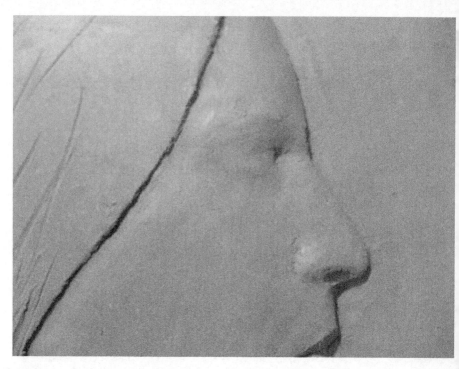

Above you can see the eyebrow and the eye mass ready to be shaped to form the eye.

Measure and check once again the correct dimensions and position of the eye with respect to the elements of the face.

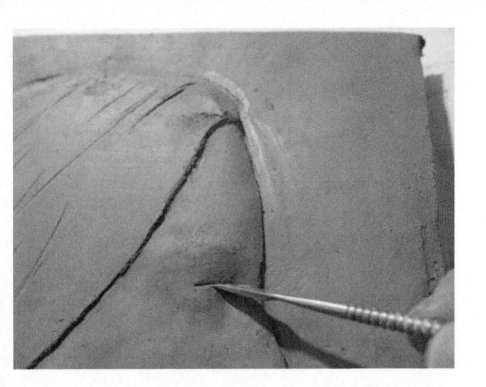

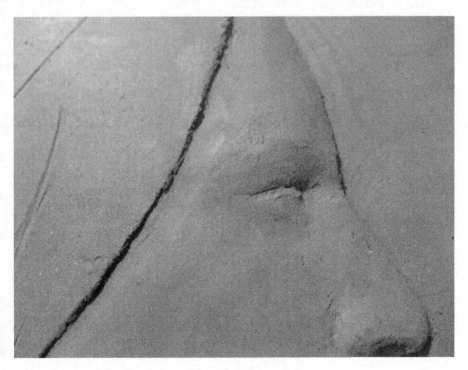

Start shaping the upper eyelid with the spatula.

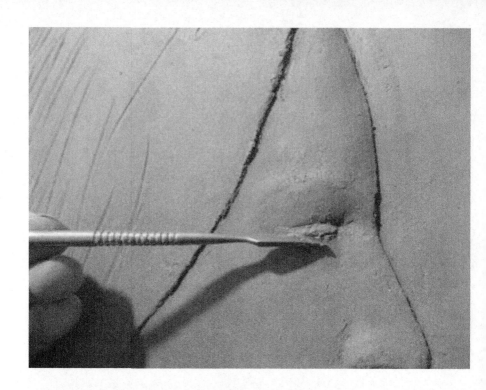

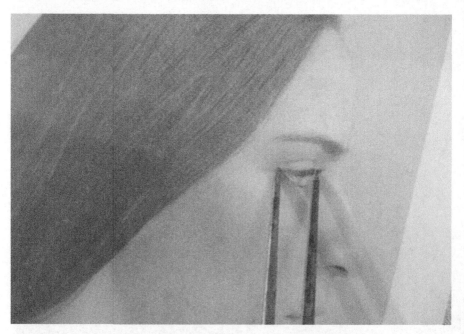

Compare the dimensions of the picture and the portrait.

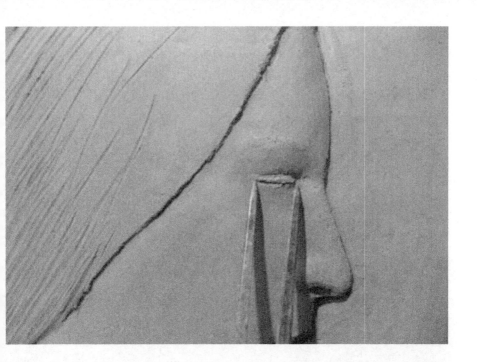

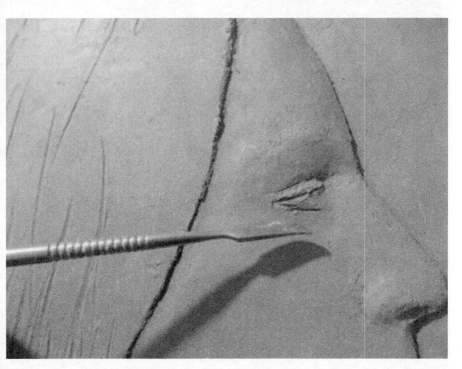

Now start forming the entire eye by making a cut that coincides with the lower eyelid.

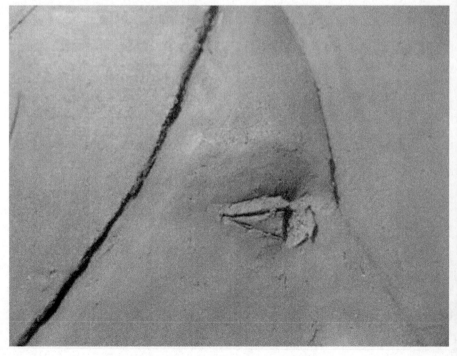

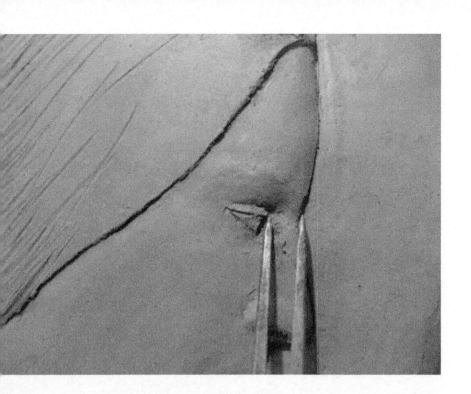

Check once more the correct dimensions and position.

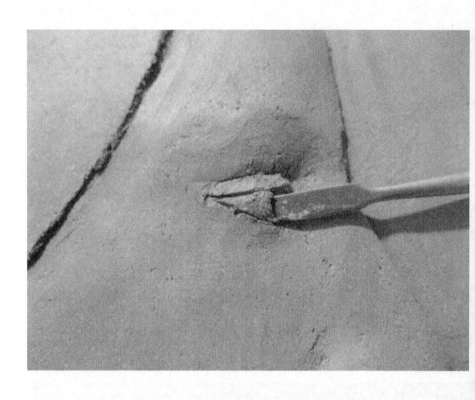

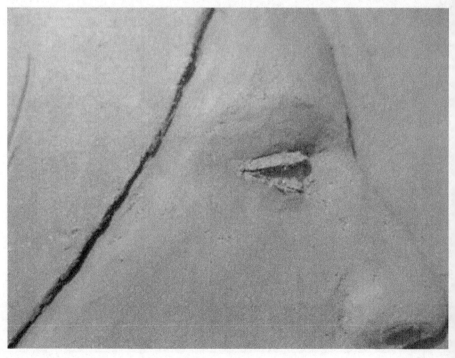

Remove a layer of clay between the cut of the upper and lower eyelid by about a millimeter in depth, in order to form the eyeball.

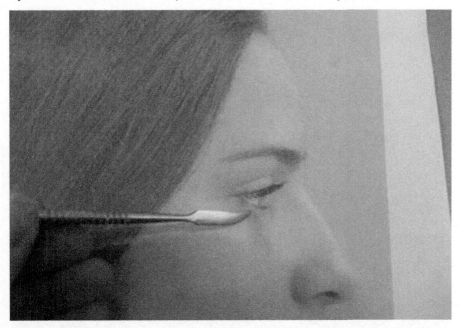

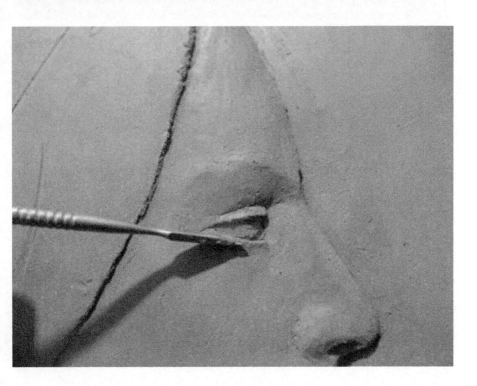

Compare your result with the picture and check the right curvature of the eyelashes.

After you have finished outlining the facial elements, you can complete the hair.

With a pointed spatula, mark furrows of varying depth so as to simulate movement and hair effect.

At this point the work is almost finished, we still need to check all the details of the portrait. However, before doing this I strongly recommend taking a break for a couple of days at least, so that your eyes and mind can rest.

It is common knowledge that by focusing for a long time on a creation, our mind can no longer distinguish any errors. Therefore, now that it is necessary to verify incredibly small and imperceptible differences between our portrait and the figure of reference in the pictures, it is appropriate to face this examination on a clear mind. Cover your work with a nylon sheet and wait at least a couple of days.

After the rest days, check and compare the dimensions of all the elements of the portrait with the compass. It is very likely that, as it happened to me, you will realize that you need to correct some details.

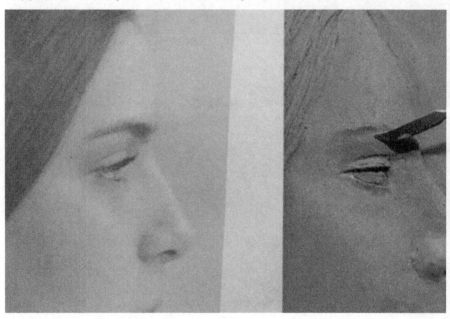

To facilitate the comparison, move the picture closer and place it on the portrait.

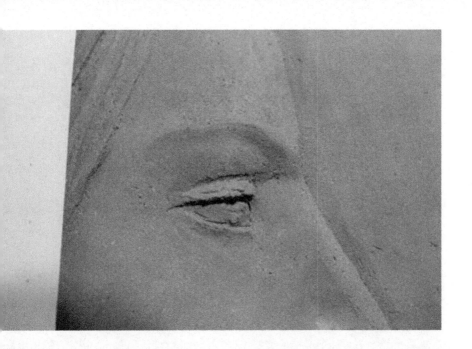

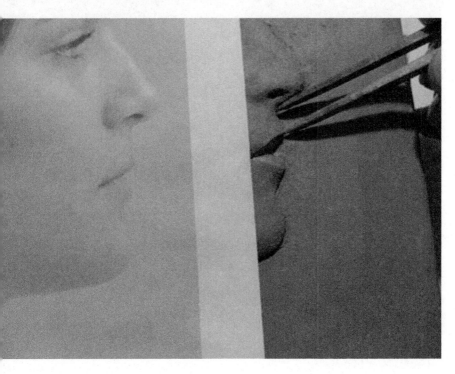

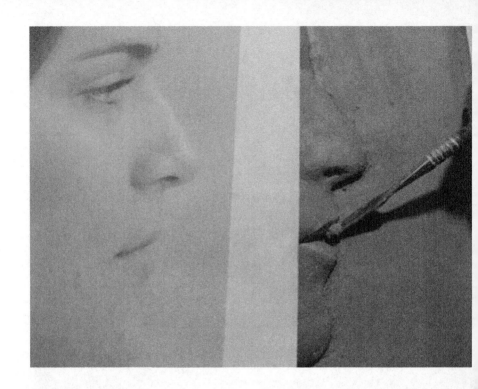

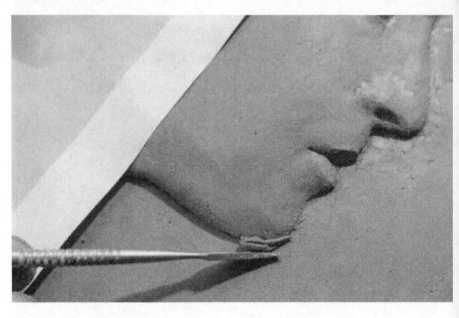

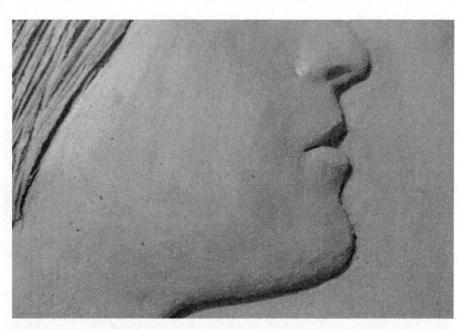

After meticulously checking everything, I noticed that there were some inaccuracies in my portrait. For example the brow, which should have been slightly fuller, the upper lip, which should have been about a millimeter longer and lastly the chin, which should have been more stretched. I polished the surfaces and shaped better the muscles of the neck, the cheeks etc.

The last optional operation is rounding the sharp edges of the clay plate.

Take the wooden rod and move it closer to the edges, pressing lightly and rotating it as you can see in the pictures below; do this on all sides.

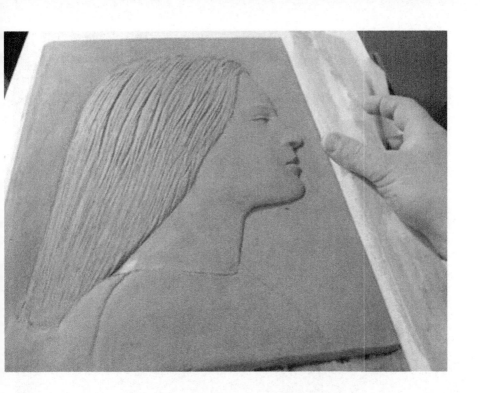

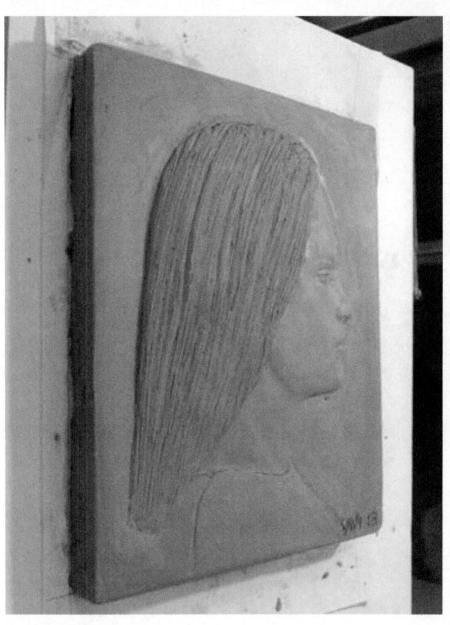

Rounded edges.

Now sign your work.

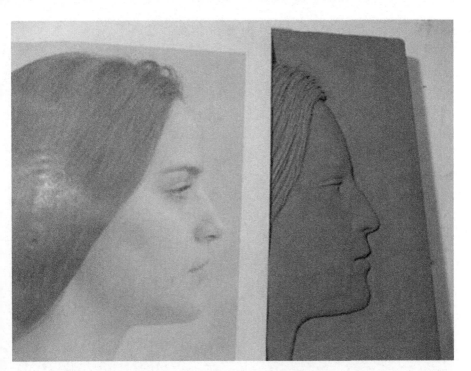

The portrait is finally finished. Just to make sure, move the picture closer and check the similarity of your clay portrait.

In the two pictures below you can see the portrait baked in the kiln at 970°C. As you can notice, the colour of the clay changed from gray to white, moreover I'd like to point out how the position of the light source is crucial for a vision of the work that highlights the anatomical shapes.

In the first of the examples below the light source is behind the head and almost in a grazing position with respect to the figure, while in the second the light source is above the head, but still raking.

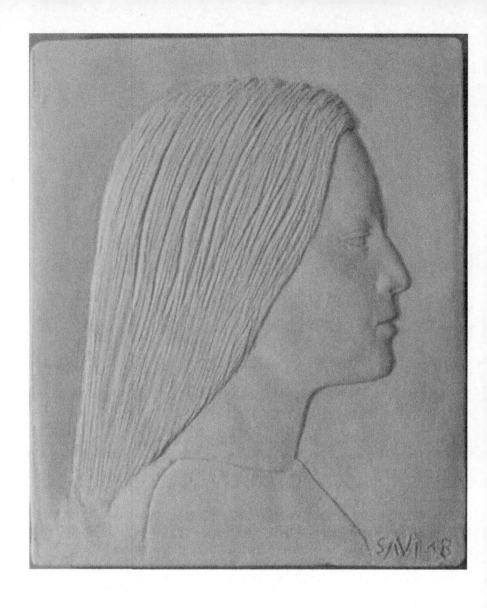

BAKING

Some baking advice.

Whether you use a gas oven, or an electric oven, I recommend a very slow baking.

Before putting it in the oven, wait until your portrait is well dried. Remember that the clay is very thick and will therefore take a long time for the innermost clay to dry completely. Obviously, it will take longer in a cold and humid environment and less time in a hot and dry environment. Either way, I recommend waiting at least a month in a hot and dry environment.

When baking, the most critical phase, which requires more attention, concerns the passage between room temperature and 500°C. As a matter of fact, even if your portrait is well dried, the mass of clay you put inside the oven will contain humidity up to a temperature of about 450°C.

Therefore, up to a temperature of 450 - 500°C, the humidity must be able to evaporate and get out of the innermost layers of the clay very slowly, otherwise the 'pressure cooker' effect will take place and some parts of the clay will break off or even explode. You would actually risk finding your creation in pieces.

Electric ovens are very practical because they have a computer with which you can program all the baking phases moment by moment.

I personally utilize a small electric oven (or kiln) with an internal size of 40 X 40 X 55 cm. It has a computer which divides the baking time in 18 parts (or stages). To each part or stage, we can assign the temperature that the kiln must reach, and the time it must employ to get there.

For example: for my portrait, I programmed the kiln so that in the first stage it reaches the temperature of 50°C in 4 hours; in the second stage it reaches the temperature of 75°C in 4 hours, in the third stage it reaches the temperature of 100°C in 3 hours and so on. As the temperature increases, a shorter amount of time is assigned to each stage. The whole 18 stages take no less than 48 - 50 hours to get to 970°C.

f you follow these instructions and you use good refractory clay, I assure you that your creation will get out of the kiln safe and sound.

For my portrait I used white refractory clay with a chamotte percentage of 40% and a maximum grain size of 1.5 mm.

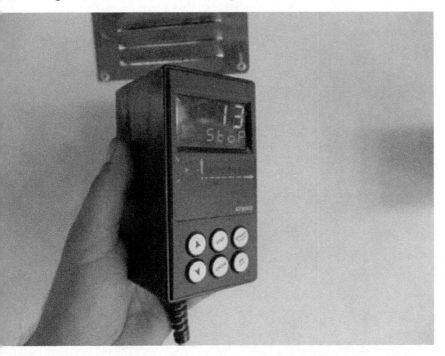

In the picture above you can see the kiln's programmable computer, which controls the temperature and the baking time.

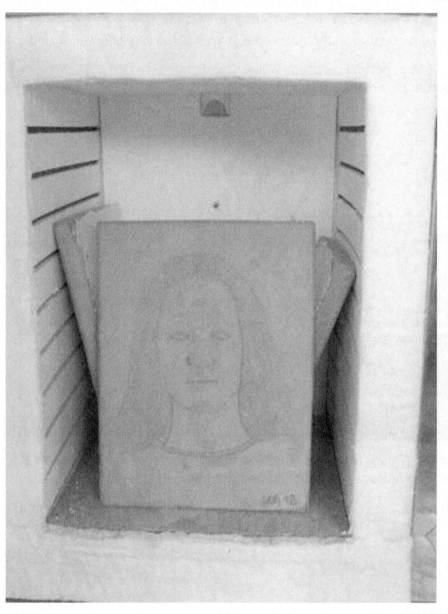

This picture shows the position of the three engraved reliefs. When placing the pieces inside the kiln it is important that the heat is distributed evenly and can envelop the objects.

Two reliefs are placed on the sides, and we can see their back and the white of the paper we had placed so as not to let the clay stick to the board. The third relief is leaning on the other two.

In the picture below you can see the works already cooked at 970° Celsius.

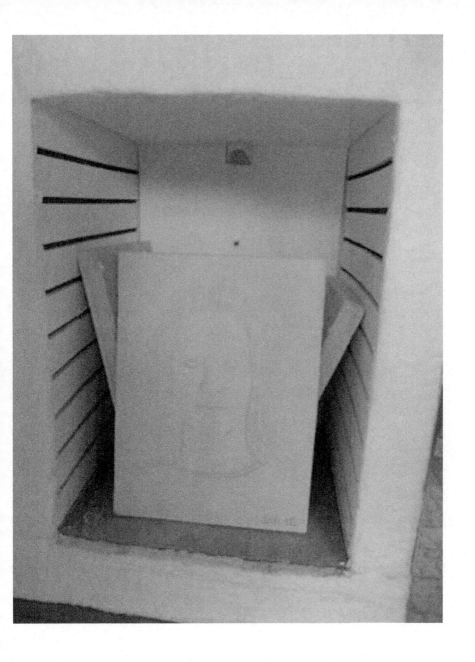

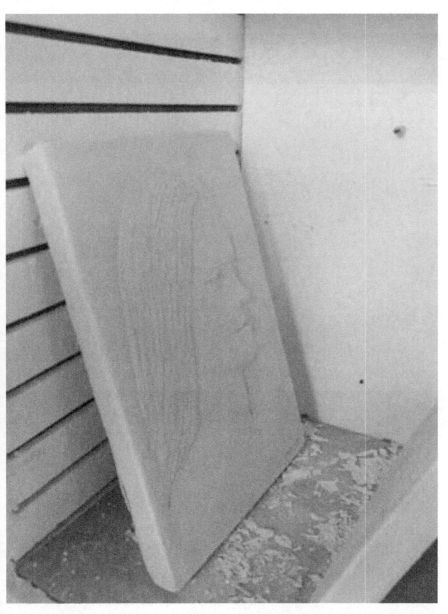

In this picture, at the base of the kiln, you can see the ash from the paper that had remained attached to the back of the reliefs.

With this last step the work is complete.

I wish you all the best in your work.

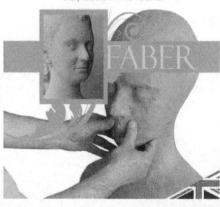

120

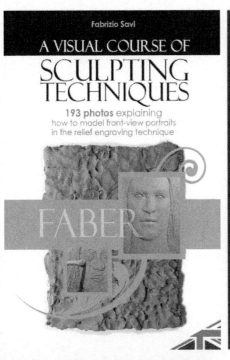

Fabrizio Savi

A VISUAL COURSE OF
SCULPTING TECHNIQUES

193 photos explaining
how to model front-view portraits
in the relief engraving technique

FABER

FABRIZIO SAVI

Model Making: A Visual Course

235 commented photos on how to use
plasticine, silicone rubber, and modeling plaster
to create 3D prototypes

FABRIZIO SAVI

How to use polyester resin :
A practical visual manual

Art experiments incorporating various colors and materials

Printed in Great Britain
by Amazon

44054572R00069